The old-time pamphlet  ost
challenging work being ess
is devoted to giving ser t's
right and what's wrong ̆ ̆e
world, including what's ̆lt
is intellectuals unbound, ̆strained and creative
texts about meaningful matters.

> "Long live Prickly Paradigm Press.... Long may its
> flaming pamphlets lift us from our complacency."
> —Ian Hacking

Prickly Paradigm is marketed and distributed by
The University of Chicago Press.

www.press.uchicago.edu

A list of current and future titles can be found on our
website and at the back of this pamphlet.

www.prickly-paradigm.com

Executive Publisher
Marshall Sahlins

Publishers
Peter Sahlins
Ramona Naddaff
Seminary Co-op Bookstore

Editor
Matthew Engelke
info@prickly-paradigm.com

Design and layout by Daniel Murphy.

The Gift Paradigm

The Gift Paradigm:
A Short Introduction to the Anti-utilitarian Movement in the Social Sciences

Alain Caillé

Translated by Gordon Connell and François Gauthier

PRICKLY PARADIGM PRESS
CHICAGO

Prickly Paradigm Press, LLC
5629 South University Avenue
Chicago, IL 60637

www.prickly-paradigm.com

ISBN: 9780996635592
LCCN: 2020941169

Printed in the United States of America on acid-free paper.

Contents

Foreword and Acknowledgments

When we created the *Mouvement anti-utilitariste dans les sciences sociales* (Anti-utilitarian Movement in the Social Sciences), in 1981, and decided to launch a journal (*Le Bulletin du MAUSS*), we immediately received the warm support of prominent intellectuals like Albert Hirschman and Charles Taylor. But the most influential author for us, after Marcel Mauss and Karl Polanyi, of course, was Marshall Sahlins, whose *Stone Age Economics* appeared to us to be a milestone (if I may say so) and an example of what had to be done in the social sciences. We regularly sent him issues of the *Bulletin du MAUSS*, without ever knowing whether he found any interest in it. So, it is not only a great honor but also a great pleasure to see one of my books published by him in his beautiful collection. It is a useful publication, too, I must confess. *La Revue du MAUSS* (as the publication became known in 1988) is a rather peculiar thing indeed, a sort of nonidentified academic object. We belong to no particular discipline—to neither anthropology nor economics nor political philosophy nor sociology—or to all of them. For this reason, we have never received any academic subsidy, but have still managed to survive through the interest not only of peripheral academics but also of the *informed reader* within the larger public. With time the MAUSS has slowly gained some academic recognition, albeit in a rather paradoxical way. We are recognized and appreciated in France by anthropologists, sociologists, economists, and philosophers, and also by historians, geographers, and psychoanalysts... as long as we do not pretend to be specialists in their fields.

The reason I am particularly pleased about this translation is that if *La Revue du MAUSS* is now well known, not just in France but also in Italy and Brazil (and to a lesser extent in Germany and Japan), it is not at all well known in the English-speaking world. I have sometimes been tempted to believe that the reason for this is that it is impossible to present oneself as anti-utilitarian in this world. But that hypothesis does not hold, since Marshall Sahlins is plainly and beyond any hint of a doubt anti-utilitarian. All the same, I never cared very much about this lack of recognition in English. I was trained as a scholar when French was still an important academic language in the social sciences. But that is not the case anymore. To enter the worldwide sphere of intellectual discussion it is nowadays mandatory to publish in English. So, I am very grateful to Marshall Sahlins for giving me and my MAUSS friends this opportunity.

This book is the slightly rewritten version of a lecture given at the Université de Paris Ouest Nanterre La Défense on October 23, 2013, at the invitation of Albert Piette, director of the Presses universitaires de Paris Nanterre, whom I would like to thank warmly for thus having given me the opportunity to bring together in a small format a whole set of theses and analyses that were otherwise somewhat scattered. The result seems to me to be a good—and highly needed—introduction to anti-utilitarianism and the "gift paradigm." However, I must apologize for one thing. The question I was asked by the organizer of the lecture was what brought *me* to anti-utilitarianism, why *I* made this choice and for what reason. I had to answer in a personal way and to say quite often *I* or *me*, which I usually dislike. I only hope, these reservations notwithstanding, that that makes the text sound livelier, especially to an English-speaking audience.

Because the publisher's choice was to bring out a small book, as accessible as possible, I thought it wise to drastically limit bibliographical references. Even if I had confined myself to my own texts, this book would have been seriously burdened, and it would have doubled in volume if I had had to quote the works to which it refers, directly or indirectly. The main disadvantage of this choice is that it does not allow me to properly discharge my debt to my friends in the MAUSS, who are quoted too furtively, and without whom none of the ideas formulated here could have seen the light of day, if only because they are often the refraction of their own ideas. They are too numerous to mention, but Philippe Chanial, Francesco Fistetti, Anne-Marie Fixot, François Flahault, François iv

Gauthier, Jacques Godbout, Roberte Hamayon, Paulo Henrique Martins, Ahmet Insel, Serge Latouche, Christian Laval, Jean-Louis Laville, Ilana Silber, Camille Tarot, and Frédéric Vandenberghe, as well as, formerly, Sylvain Dzimira, and, more recently, Simon Borel and Pierre Prades, will recognize more particularly than others what I owe them here.

PS: Ah! I almost forgot. It goes without saying that my friends in the MAUSS are in no way responsible for any inaccuracies or errors that may be discovered in this text.

Introduction

The request addressed to me by Nanterre's university press to explain for what purpose—*pour quoi*, and not *pourquoi* (why)—I did what I did, wrote what I wrote, and thought what I tried to think under the aegis of anti-utilitarianism and the gift paradigm is very difficult to honor: it would mean, were I to take it totally seriously, to probe my deepest intentions, to carry out a sort of examination of conscience, and hence to try to "say everything." Mission impossible, of course. Reflecting on my journey from this angle, from this question, the first thing that came to mind was an aphorism published in an astonishing book, *Propos d'O. L. Barenton, confiseur* (Remarks by O L. Barenton, confectioner), by Auguste Detœuf, great leader of French employers in the pre–World War II period. Barenton/Detœuf asks himself, What are we working for? When you are young, he writes—and I quote from memory—you imagine that you are working for yourself. Later, you imagine you are working for your wife and children. And finally, after spending one's life working, one realizes that one is working to work. Paraphrasing, I would be tempted to answer the question of "Why anti-utilitarianism and the gift paradigm" thus: so that there may be anti-utilitarianism and a gift paradigm.

If I had to summarize in a less lapidary way my career path and what I believe to be its reasons for being, I would say that the essence of what I have tried to do over the past thirty years or so has been to fight, within my means, against the growing hegemony of the economy on the world, or against its reduction to the sole dimension of a market economy. And more precisely, today, against its reduction to a speculative and rentier market economy, which sometimes maintains more or less tangible links with criminal and mafia-like financial networks in opaque tax havens.

This fight, however, is not that of an activist but of an academic. What links the two types of fight is how the economic and speculative transformation of the world can in large part be traced to the upheaval that occurred thirty or forty years ago in the fields of social sciences and political philosophy: an upheaval that ended up handing over a preeminent—and increasingly hegemonic—place to the discourse of economists. If economics has triumphed, it is because the representatives of other disciplines—philosophers, sociologists, anthropologists, historians, and so forth—have not been able to build an intellectual edifice strong enough to plausibly and effectively oppose the monopoly of legitimate discourse and practice in social science that has been conquered by economists and, in their wake, by financiers and traders.

I will outline this general idea in three stages. In the first, I return to the work done by the *Revue du MAUSS* in its first ten years; this was an almost exclusively critical period, which can be described as anti-utilitarian or anti-economicist. In the second, I ask what can be opposed to the generalized economic vulgate. I and my friends in the MAUSS call this, among other things, the gift paradigm (*paradigme du don*), by which we designate a way of conceiving the essence of the social bond as other than the one that dominates today. Finally, in a third stage, I conclude with some of the ethical and political issues at stake in this reflection.

Chapter 1
Why *La Revue du MAUSS* and Why Anti-utilitarianism

La Revue du MAUSS (Journal of the anti-utilitarian movement in the social sciences), whose name also pays tribute to Marcel Mauss, was created in 1981, following the observation by some of us economists, sociologists, and anthropologists of a drift that affected both the social sciences and political philosophy. This drift consisted of a disruption in the division of intellectual labor. For about two centuries—let us say, symbolically, since 1776—when Adam Smith's *The Wealth of Nations* was published, economists had confined themselves to studying the functioning of the market, specifically the fields of production, distribution, and consumption of wealth. To this end, they made the pledge that the *Homo economicus* model—that is, the hypothesis that human subjects are individual calculators, mutually indifferent, interested only in their own needs or preferences, and considered to be more or less rational—was sufficiently relevant and effective to explain what happens in the market for goods and services. In decisions to buy or sell. As concerns the rest, they abandoned its study to the other disciplines. As Vilfredo Pareto (who was famous as both an economist and a sociologist) said, alongside the *Homo economicus*, there is room for the study of *Homo politicus*, *Homo religiosus*, and so on.

Generalized Economicism

However, from the 1960s to the 1970s, some economists, gradually joined by the majority in the discipline, came to think that their explanatory model could be applied to other fields of social life, even those in which there is neither trade nor, consequently, formation of market prices. Why not suppose, they asked, that it is in all areas of social existence, and not only in the economy, that we act as individual, selfish, and rational calculators, seeking only to maximize our own interest? From there, and notably with the work of Gary Becker, a future Nobel Prize winner in economics, began the proliferation of a large number of studies on the profitability of, for example:

- higher education: What is the relationship between the investment made and the expected future gains?
- marriage: Is it worth getting married? What does it generate financially, at what discount rate per year?

- love or crime: What is gained by loving? Can crime pay? What is the profitability calculation, the criminal's business plan?
- religion: Is it profitable to believe in God? Let us remember, moreover, in this sense and emerging well before the contemporary generalized economic model, Pascal's wager, which was based on the argument that believing in God does not cost much and that it can yield a lot. An infinite gain! It is this thesis of Pascal's that the new economic model generalizes.

What struck me and many of my friends in the 1980s was that this general utilitarian model triumphed not only among economists but in other disciplines that had hitherto strongly opposed it, including sociology. Worse, it triumphed even among those whose opposition to this vision of the social bond had been their raison d'être. Let us refer, for example, to the sociology of the 1970s and 1980s in France. Three of the discipline's four principal authors of the time—Raymond Boudon, Pierre Bourdieu, Michel Crozier, and Alain Touraine—began to consider sociology as a particular form of a generalized economic model. This is the case with Raymond Boudon, herald of rational choice theory and methodological individualism, which constitute economists' basic methodological and epistemological posture. But this is also the case, on the anti-liberal side, of Pierre Bourdieu, who presents his sociology as a "general economy of practice." In other words, and even though it rests on post-Marxist and post-Freudian bases, Bourdieu's theory entails the application of the economic model and its maximizing calculus to all spheres of social practice, if only operating on an unconscious and collective rather than purely individual level. Michel Crozier, writing with Erhard Friedberg, advocated a "strategic analysis" of organizations that aimed to reveal the power "interests" of the various groups struggling in the business world. Only Alain Touraine at the time did not participate in this evolution.

There has been a similar recourse to the generalized economic model in political philosophy, where John Rawls's great 1971 work, *A Theory of Justice*, which occupied center stage throughout the entire late twentieth century, posed the political question in the very language of economists: How are we to define the norms of a just society, assuming that human subjects are only ordinary, mutually indifferent individuals, each acting as a *Homo economicus*? And there, too, rational choice theory was the basic language, the lingua franca of the most prominent political philosophers of the time, Anglo-Saxons for the most part, who wondered whether to extend Rawls's work or to criticize it.

In those years, one could feel the surge of the generalized economic model in the social sciences as well as in moral and political philosophy. It took about ten years for us in the MAUSS to understand that this intellectual revolution had ultimately preceded and promoted evolutions in the real world. It is this intellectual revolution (or counterrevolution) that has made *globalization* intellectually and ideologically possible. Globalization, which must not be understood as the internationalization of markets and cultures as much as the worldwide generalization of the commercial, speculative, and financialized norm of the market to all spheres of human existence. One only had to convince oneself that human beings indeed act as nothing more than *Homo economicus*, and that the only thing that interests them is the maximization of their individual interests, to conceive of the market as the only efficient and legitimate form of coordination between individuals or collectives. If we are all only *Homo economicus*, then the only intelligent thing to do, the only "rational" procedure, is indeed to aim to maximize our financial capital as quickly as possible, and to resort to speculation if it is not too risky. Starting from the proposition that markets are "efficient," it follows that the more we invest in the stock market, the richer we will become.

Such was the starting point for the *Revue du MAUSS*: the opposition to this strange, disconcerting, and in part deleterious evolution of modern thought and of the division of intellectual labor in the social sciences and political philosophy.

A Certain Vision of Sociology

1. But why did I embark on this adventure? Probably because the course of my academic studies turned out to be more singular than I thought at the time. After studying economics and sociology simultaneously, I first obtained a doctorate in economics, in 1974. But, having read at a very early stage—thanks to my sociology studies—Mauss's *The Gift*, I was at once sensitive to the extraordinary contrast that exists between the basic postulates of economists and what one reads in anthropology. I was also, at a very young age, appointed assistant to Claude Lefort, philosopher and sociologist, intellectual heir to Maurice Merleau-Ponty. Lefort, who died in 2010, was one of the leading contemporary thinkers on democracy and, with Hannah Arendt, one of the greatest analysts of totalitarian regimes. By a quirk of history, I was waiting for an assistant position in economics when he offered me an assistant position in sociology at the University of Caen. When I first met him, two years earlier, I had been preparing a thesis in sociology under the supervision of Raymond Aron. The title of the thesis was "Planification as the Ideology of Bureaucracy." It was in this context that I had read texts by Lefort in the journal *Socialisme ou Barbarie*, whose three most prominent authors were Lefort, Cornelius Castoriadis, and Jean-François Lyotard.

2. Without knowing it, by becoming Lefort's assistant, I became acquainted with what seems to me today the French equivalent of the Frankfurt School. Both schools of thought were created and animated

by authors who had been Marxists (Trotskyists, in the French case) and who tried to reflectively realize their exit from Marxism, or to overcome some of its impasses, its assumptions or its mistakes, while keeping alive an ideal of both thought and emancipation.

It would be very interesting, by the way, to engage in a somewhat systematic comparison between the *Socialisme ou Barbarie* group and the Frankfurt School, of Adorno and Horkheimer in their early days, and of their successors Habermas and, today, Axel Honneth. These two schools of thought share at least two fundamental ideas to which I have remained faithful and which largely explain the work of the *Revue du MAUSS*.

The first is that there is no sense in separating social sciences from political philosophy. A resolutely interdisciplinary approach is needed in both fields. And besides, in the wake of the foundation of the sociology department by Lefort at the University of Caen, in 1967, the dominant choice has been to teach sociologists not only sociology (in the narrow sense of the term), but also anthropology, psychoanalysis, political economy, and history.

The second is that academic reflection cannot and should not be separated from ethical and political commitment.

The articulation between these two ideas was extended, after *Socialisme ou Barbarie*, in other journals, in particular *Textures* and *Libre*. It inspired some of the main contemporary French philosophers, all students or heirs, direct or indirect, of Lefort, such as Marcel Gauchet, Pierre Rosanvallon, Miguel Abensour, Pierre Manent, and Myriam Revault d'Allonnes.

8

Let us not forget that the choice to follow these ideas—of interdisciplinarity and of the assumed link between social science and ethical and political commitment—does not stem only from Marxism. It is also a legacy of the French sociological tradition, notably that of Auguste Comte and Émile Durkheim. Just remember Durkheim's famous phrase in his preface to the first edition of *The Division of Labor in Society* (1893): "We would esteem our research not worth the labor of a single hour if its interest were merely speculative." In other words, sociology only makes sense if it feeds the political. It is therefore a question, to capture it in a formula, and against a certain Weberian tradition (that misunderstands Weber, by the way), of being both scientific and political. It is this principle that continues to animate the *Revue du MAUSS* and to inspire my conception of sociology. A principle that is very different from the one that dominates the discipline today.

3. Let us therefore go back a little, to note that sociology, from its origins, has had grandiose ambitions that we must now recognize have not been satisfied.[1] These ambitions have long since faded considerably. Sociology now sees itself, and is perceived from the outside, as a specialized social science among others, a social science confined to what is left, to the study of what other social sciences do not talk about and leave aside for it to seize. Greatness and decadence! Sociology nowadays talks about only what economists, philosophers, historians, and anthropologists do not talk about. Largely renouncing its theoretical ambitions (outsourced to philosophers), it sees itself—and

wants to see itself—increasingly as a simple fieldwork science, radically empirical. It thus abandons its original theoretical ideal.[2]

And yet this ideal was extraordinarily ambitious, in the good sense of the term, and promising: sociology was to be at the crossroads of all the disciplines in social sciences and take up questions of moral and political philosophy, only differently. As their other face. The questions that moral and political philosophers approached from an essentially conceptual and speculative perspective, sociologists tried to (re)formulate by privileging an empirical approach. However, these two faces cannot function independently of each other. Consequently, sociology, as I see it, must be, together with moral and political philosophy, the generalist discipline of the social sciences.[3] Or rather, their generalist, interdisciplinary, and dialogical moment. Since sociology no longer presents itself in this way and since *sociology* now designates something other than what it meant in the beginning, it is better to talk about reviving the project of a *general social science* (a *social science* and *social theory* in the singular) in which ethnologists, as well as historians, economists, philosophers (and sociologists...), and so forth might recognize themselves.[4]

On Some Prerequisites for a General Social Science (or General Sociology)

How can we try to hold on to such a project? By paying due attention to what I believe are the four methodological and epistemological imperatives of social science or, if we prefer, of a general sociology.

- The first imperative, the one that differentiates social science from moral and political philosophy, is the empirical one, the *description* of reality, whether through observation or experimentation. Indeed, there is no conceivable scientific claim for social science without the aim of establishing and recording the facts.

- The second imperative is the imperative of *explanation*. Of showing the "reasons" of phenomena. No science is possible, here again, without research into the causes that produce the phenomena that we have described. Here, we must ask the question *why* (that of the *Weil-Motiven*, in the words of the phenomenologist sociologist Alfred Schutz), to eventually be able to make predictions through modeling. That is how economists proceed. But this is also true of the structural anthropology of Claude Lévi-Strauss, for example, when, from the study of certain South American Indian myths, he deduces the probable existence of a certain mythical form, not yet discovered, in North America.

- Let us call the third imperative interpretative or hermeneutical, which encourages us to ask the question *for what*, *for which purpose* (that of Schutz's *Um-zu-Motiven*). In order to do what, for which ends do social actors do what they do? They act because they have reasons to act that must be questioned. Reasons that make sense to them. Reasons, not just causes. What are the values that drive social subjects to act? Such is what must be understood through *interpretation*.

- The fourth imperative can be described as *normative*, or *axiological*. Researchers cannot interrogate the values that motivate social subjects without questioning their own values. Social science must not limit itself to questioning what makes sense for the actors it observes and analyses. It must also and at the same time ask what makes sense for itself and therefore also consider which values, and for what purpose, social scientists decide to get involved in the social sciences.

Once those distinctions have been made, we can try to go ahead and elucidate the conditions for a possible general social science. Let us insist on five points.

1. Contrary to the current methodological vulgates, it is essential to understand that the normative impera- tive, the obligation that the descriptions, explanations, and interpretations produced make sense for scholars, or in other words for a "universal audience," is the most important of the four methodological and episte- mological imperatives in social science. Compliance is the very condition of their cognitive fertility. It is only insofar as they are driven by normative issues (ethical,

ideological, or political) that scholarly investigations feed a fruitful process of thought and research. Yet the social sciences, in their current state, on the contrary, foreclose this normative commitment in the name of a largely erroneous and misleading imperative of axiological neutrality.

2. If we take seriously the idea that, in the social sciences, the normative imperative is structuring—which in no way means that scholars should limit themselves to stating their opinions, since they can only be considered scholarly if they know how to go through the course of description, explication, interpretation, and axiological reflexivity—then it is possible to deduce a certain methodological approach that can be asserted as a counterpoint and complement to Max Weber's famous ideal-typical method. For him, the privileged tool of social science is the construction of ideal types, constructed in principle according to a certain idea of instrumental rationality. In this context, one wonders what agents considered rational from the point of view of instrumental rationality (*Zweckrationalität*) would have done, and why they are not in reality as rational as they could have been.

It seems interesting to me to construct a symmetrical approach that I would gladly call *typical-idealistic*, or typically idealistic, which would start not from rationality in relation to means but from rationality in relation to values (*Wertrationalität*). You can act rationally, Weber explains, because you do it in the name of the values you cherish, even if it's not effective from an instrumental point of view, and even if you don't personally benefit from doing it. One can be a rational fool, as Amartya Sen puts it, who sacrifices one's personal utility and well-being to the accomplishment of certain ethical or political ends. The same can be true of countries, collectives, or institutions, which sacrifice a share of instrumental (particularly economic) efficiency for the benefit of their values. But just as social actors are never fully rational in their search for instrumental or utilitarian effectiveness—and one has to ask why—so they are not always (or they are rarely) perfectly consistent with their own values. With their ideal self (*Ideal Ich*).

Why do social actors never fully realize the values according to which they believe or claim to act, and believe or claim to profess? This question, specific to the typical-idealistic approach, implies a double task: to make explicit all the values in question by taking them truly seriously, and to ask why they are not respected. And what prevents their realization. It is an approach of this type that animated one of MAUSS's struggles around the idea of an unconditional minimum income, which seemed to us to be the logical outcome of human rights.[5] If we take the values of human rights seriously, then we should logically end up with such a proposition. Why, then, is this not done? What's against it?

3. If we want to effectively go beyond the generalized economic model that dominates both sociological thought and social practice, we must therefore elucidate the possible foundations of a generalist social science that cannot be reduced to the economy. But the question that then arises is, Why have all the attempts to construct a general sociology, until now,

failed? Why do economists, from all schools of thought, share the same set of central concepts, in almost every university in the world, while in the social sciences, and in sociology in particular, we are confronted with an infinite plurality of schools of thought all launching attacks at each other, leading to their general common impotence? For two fundamental reasons.

The first is that all systems constructed by classical sociology have presented themselves as systematic sociologies. As *systems*, precisely, except in Weber. This is the case, for example, in what C. Wright Mills ironically called Talcott Parsons's "grand theory," which divided the social system into small boxes, sub-boxes, sub-sub-boxes, and so on. As it is with Niklas Luhmann and his theory of the "autopoietic social system"; with Bourdieu and his "general economy of practice"; or with James Coleman and his methodological individualism in the *Foundations of Social Theory*. This is the case also, in some respects, in the theory of justification of Luc Boltanski and Laurent Thévenot, with its five + *n* cities.

These general sociologies, whatever their merits may be otherwise, do not do justice to reality, since they claim to have a systematic answer to everything. With them, we know in advance what we must find, in which theoretical box, under which concept or under which preexisting heading we will put what we have observed. We know in advance, for example, that social reality can be divided, without remnants, in well-defined orders or systems. Or that it is built on rational individual choices. Or that societies are organized, on the contrary, as a priori totalities, with society preexisting itself and the actors then only applying social values (as culturalism holds), performing functions (according to functionalism), or obeying rules (posits structuralism). It seems to me that we need to go beyond these sociological systems that claim to have answers to everything, by proposing flexible concepts that allow us to ask good questions rather than have an answer ready *for everything*. Both empirical and theoretical questions. Yet it is true that asking relevant questions, the right questions, of course, makes it possible to anticipate the right answers.

4. The second reason for the failure of general inherited sociologies is that systematic sociologies have not sufficiently grasped the fact that the main challenge facing sociology is to think about its relationship to economics and political economy, as well as to the utilitarian foundations of economics. I repeat here, by completing it and systematizing it slightly, Christian Laval's analysis in *L'Ambition sociologique*, which is, in my opinion, undoubtedly the best existing history of sociology, parallel but superior to Robert Nisbet's *The Sociological Tradition*.[6]

    In their relationship to economics, the great classical sociologists have generally experienced four stages in their trajectory of thought. The first is usually *approval*. The first sociologists, and in particular Saint-Simon, Marx, and Weber, were initially amazed by political economy, which was the first social science constituted, the one that seemed to give an objective analysis of social reality; it was, moreover, not only objective but also quantifiable in principle, on the model of Newtonian mechanics. But very quickly comes the second stage, *objection*. Yes, the models produced by economists are grandiose and seductive, but the anthropology on which they are based, the model of *Homo economicus*, is not tenable, according to sociologists. Social actors are not just needy beings seeking to maximize their individual satisfaction and capital. Something else comes into play: affects, passions, values, ideology, the weight of tradition and society.

The third stage is *objectification*, starting with an attempt to objectify the objectivity of economic discourse. To produce a sort of second-level objectification. A meta-objectification. It is then a question—and especially for Marx or Weber—of showing, thanks to a historicizing approach, that all the economic categories that economists consider to be natural and eternal are in reality the more or less recent result of historical constructions. And this is also true of philosophical categories, and also of all social representations, as Durkheim powerfully suggests. Following the thread of this type of reasoning leads to the current fashion of radical constructivism: everything is built; therefore, everything can be deconstructed, we are told, and we can, or even must, build something else. But build what?

5. This is where we reach the fourth stage of the ideal-typical path of the classical sociologist, with the attempt *to surpass* economic science not only through its critique but also with respect to positivity. What anthropology could be opposed to the figure of the *Homo economicus*? If the primary or sole motor of social action is not, or not only, need, what is it? Classical sociologists as a whole, and each in their own way, have tried to go beyond the economic explanation by sooner

or later arriving at the idea that the essence or matrix of social phenomena is to be found in religion. Marx himself, at a certain moment, places at the heart of capitalism the fetishism of the commodity, that religion of the commodity without which the system of capital could not hold and self-reproduce. It is the same thing with the epistemological metamorphosis of Durkheim, who, following a sort of hallucination or revelation, discovered in 1895 that religion is the first moment and the very basis of social life. Or with Weber and his gigantic work on the comparative historical sociology of religion.

The only problem is that nobody really knows what religion is. What it consists of. Neither sociologists nor anthropologists have ever managed to agree on a minimal definition, or even to be certain that religion is actually present in all societies.[7] In the French tradition, for more than fifty years, reference to religion has been replaced by the evocation or invocation of the "symbolic," which serves as a philosopher's stone for certain structuralist anthropologists and Lacanian psychoanalysts. But nobody is able to agree on a shared definition of the symbolic, either. Social science therefore remains blocked at this stage. To try to unblock it, we have to dig, in order to find out what is upstream of the economic model, what inspires economic science. Where do its success and its apparent self-evidence come from?

The Question of the Nature of Utilitarianism

Upstream there is utilitarianism. When we created the *Revue du MAUSS*, in 1981, we called it the "Journal of the Anti-Utilitarian Movement" without really knowing why. The choice of this name has worked as a gift from heaven, since it has inspired us for over thirty years. But we must admit that we hardly knew at the beginning exactly what *utilitarianism* meant. We well remembered that Durkheim and Mauss situated their approach explicitly and in many passages in opposition to utilitarianism. But we soon realized that the utilitarianism they were attacking was not really *utilitarianism* in the historical sense. What they were fighting against under this name was the sociology of Herbert Spencer, globally dominant in the 1880s, which was a social contract sociology of an individualistic methodological type. Or even ontological. Yet true utilitarianism, official and canonical utilitarianism, is that of Jeremy Bentham, who is universally considered to be the father of canonical utilitarianism. And this is quite different from the "utilitarianism" that Durkheim and Mauss criticized, since Bentham constantly opposes the theories of the social contract, which seem to him to be phantasmagorical, useless, and inoperative.

1. All these debates on the status of utilitarianism were completely forgotten in France in the 1980s. As we had declared ourselves anti-utilitarians—out of loyalty to Durkheim and Mauss, but also to Marx, who saw in Bentham's utilitarianism a "shopkeeper's morality"—it was up to us to take a closer look at the question.

So, paradoxically, it was we who, very largely, did the first work of exhuming utilitarian texts, just to know what we were really opposing ourselves to. Without entering into a scholarly debate on what utilitarianism ultimately is,[8] a debate that arouses many passions and highly contradictory interpretations, I will give a minimal definition of it, none other than that of Bentham himself (in his *Constitutional Code*). According to him, utilitarianism is based on three principles.

The first principle, relating to what *is*, posits that we are "self-regarding" individuals, concerned about ourselves, seeking to maximize our pleasures and minimize our pains. The second principle, potentially antithetical to the first, relates to justice and what *ought to be*. According to Bentham, this is just what makes it possible to obtain "the greatest happiness for the greatest number." From which it follows that if the goal is to maximize the happiness of the greatest number, then it is legitimate to achieve it by sacrificing individual interests. The first principle can be seen as an apology for calculating selfish hedonism, the second as a plea for sacrificial altruism. It is to designate the tension between these two principles that I have sometimes referred to it as the "antinomy of utilitarian reason." According to Bentham, the tension's resolution resides in a third principle relating to the desirable mode of coexistence of the first two, which Bentham calls the "means-prescribing principle" and which Élie Halévy, the great historian of classical utilitarianism, places under the register of what he calls "the artificial harmonization of interests." In order for what *is* and what *ought to be* to be compatible, it is necessary to be under the good care of a benevolent legislator who will handle punishments and rewards in a rational manner, so that the interests of all converge. This rational legislator is the equivalent of the head of the panoptic prison, invented by Bentham, the guard who knows everything, sees everything, and hears everything, and is seen by no one, according to a logic well analyzed by Michel Foucault.

2. But exactly how old is this utilitarianism? In the beginnings of the MAUSS, I thought, following the lineage of Foucault and Marx, that utilitarianism was assimilable to the ideology of the bourgeoisie that appeared in the eighteenth century. Now, on closer examination, it appears that utilitarianism is infinitely older. A significant part of ancient philosophy, and especially Plato's exoteric philosophy, as expressed in the *Protagoras*, the *Republic*, the *Laws*, or the *Gorgias*, is already totally utilitarian.[9] And this doctrine finds its equivalent in China, in the 3rd century BC, with Han Feizi, whose writings, translated into French with the title *Le Tao du Prince* (The Tao of the Prince), give us a quite explosive mixture of Plato, Adam Smith, Bentham, and Machiavelli. Utilitarianism, therefore, does not date back merely two centuries. Only its bourgeois version is recent and specifically modern; that is, the idea that the maximization of pleasure comes first through the accumulation of material wealth through the game of the market.

3. Let us examine this bourgeois version. If society is to be governed by a rational legislator who knows how to calculate everyone's pleasures and pains, in order to maximize the former and minimize the latter, they

must have a measuring instrument at their disposal to calculate these utilities. According to Bentham, there unfortunately exists no "hedonometer," no instrument for measuring pleasure. So, the best measure of what gives us pleasure is still what we would be willing to pay to get it. The right measure, the only conceivable and practicable option, is therefore money and the price of goods and services. Now, from the moment one posits that price is the adequate measure of pleasure (or utility, or preference, as you like it), one has all the foundations of the ideology of contemporary growth that is based on the idea that the gross national product (GNP) is the equivalent of gross national happiness. Thus closes the loop that makes economics the crystallization par excellence of modern utilitarianism, enabling its relative hegemony over the other social sciences, which in turn is the correlate of the domination exercised by the economic and financial sphere over all other spheres of social activities.

The strength of utilitarianism, and of the economic ideology that is its contemporary avatar, is that it seems to constitute the only possible answer to the question of what we should base the social order (or society) on, if we exclude the answers that tend to subordinate the social order to the observance of a divine, transcendent law or to the respect of tradition. Is utilitarianism the only rational answer? It all depends on what you put under the flag of reason. Let us say that utilitarianism brings a rationalist answer. It is highly doubtful that it is reasonable.

Chapter 2
The Gift Paradigm

What can be opposed to this generalized economic model and its utilitarian matrix? A lot of things: our spontaneous knowledge, the history of literature, the message of religions, poetry, art, ordinary morality, our strongest intuitions, common decency. But all this is not enough to make a set of proposals sufficiently axiomatic to serve as a basis for a generalist social science (moral and political philosophy included) and to build a discourse capable of organizing a school of political philosophy. If we restrict the field of investigation to what allows for the building of both a political alternative to neoliberalism and a scientific alternative to utilitarianism in the social sciences, then there are not many authors directly usable. The two main thinkers in this field, in addition to the great names of classical sociology or anthropology, are the historian and anthropologist Karl Polanyi, and Marcel Mauss. The

MAUSS's bet is that the greatest number of principles of this general social science that I call for can be found in Mauss's work.[10]

Mauss was the nephew and intellectual heir of Émile Durkheim, founder of French sociology. He spoke an impressive number of languages and had an absolutely encyclopedic ethnological knowledge. His students said of him: "Mauss knows everything." He wrote in 1923–24 (and published in 1925) his essential text in the history of the social sciences, both very easy and very difficult to read: *The Gift*, in which he gathers all the ethnological knowledge of his time to try to identify the general features of certain "archaic" or "early" societies. He shows that in these societies the social bond is not based on the market, on give and take, on the contract—an essential observation, since most of the philosophical thoughts of modernity are "social contract" theories—but on what he calls the triple obligation of giving, receiving, and giving back. Hence Mauss's conclusion: "The economic man is not behind us, but lies ahead."

One of the fundamental ambiguities of this text lies in the word "gift," which immediately triggers religious connotations—charity, beneficence, altruism... But that is not what Mauss is talking about. Rather, he evokes an "agonistic" gift—in which it is a question of "flattening one's rival," of putting him in the "shadow of his name"—that is to say, a challenge of generosity, which is a form of war (through the gift). But a war that has the special and precious characteristic of allowing peace to be made. The exchange of murders, beatings, insults, and wounds is substituted by the assault of generosity, by the exchange of words, precious goods, and women. The type of gift that Mauss studies in this text—explicitly leaving aside an enormous ensemble, much larger, of phenomena he calls nonagonistic "total performances" (*prestations totales*)—is an agonistic exchange that transforms enemies into allies.

What can be generalized and axiomatized from a general social science perspective that starts from here? An enormous amount of things from which I extract three series of theses or proposals concerning, respectively: first, the political; second, a theory of action; and third, a theory of religious history and the structure of modernity.

On the Political

At the end of *The Gift*, Mauss delivers, as always without making it explicit, the prolegomenon of a political philosophy that is neither contractualist nor utilitarian. The initial idea is that the decision to give one's adversaries goods, women, good words, and so on makes it possible to switch from war to peace, to transform, as we have seen, enemies into allies. This is the very essence of the political, whose gift thus appears as the primary operator. For Mauss, this operator first concerns society, but it is then possible to generalize it to interindividual relations, which are also governed by ambivalence and by the alternation of hostility and friendship. Political communities are first and foremost communities of the gift. What indeed cements the constitution of a political community, if not gifts? It is the set of gifts that we think we have received from our predecessors, from their allies, from those we recognize as our forebears. And it is, correspondingly, all those to whom one thinks one can or must give something (for example, nationality), and from whom one expects to receive something in return. It is also all those to whom we intend to bequeath or pass on something, our descendants.[11] We can therefore say that a political community is founded by the integral (in the quasi-mathematical sense of the term) of the gifts.

But to fully grasp the scale and scope of Mauss's discovery, it is necessary to generalize the theme of the triple obligation to give, receive, and give, and to do so in the context of at least four points.

1. On reflection, it appears that the triad of giving, receiving, and giving back only really makes sense if it is qualified by a fourth moment, that of demand. This moment of demand is both external—it goes beyond obligation—and internal, since without it the triple obligation to give, receive, and give back would become empty. If you give something to someone, you assume that they have a certain need, a certain desire, a certain demand. The demand could be the object of an explicit request by the donee, or simply guessed or anticipated by the donor. But is this really what is desired? Is the gift likely to satisfy the demand? Probably not, or not entirely. However, it is because there is this mismatch between gift and demand that the dynamics of the cycle are constantly being revived. The cycle of giving is therefore organized in four stages—asking, giving, receiving, and giving back. And it is important to understand that this positive symbolic cycle only makes sense against the background of its opposite, the corresponding cycle of ignoring, taking,

refusing, and keeping. The problem of a political community, of a friendly relationship, of a couple, of a team, of a company, of any organization, is to manage to pass as systematically and durably as possible from the *diabolic* cycle of ignoring, taking, refusing, and keeping to the *symbolic* cycle of asking, giving, receiving, and giving back.[12]

2. How does the symbolic dynamic of giving *work*, and more precisely, how does it engage? The starting point is to be found in what I propose to call "conditional unconditionality." No political community, organization, or friendly or loving relationship is possible without a desire and an unconditional first acceptance to be together, which exceeds and precedes any contract. When two societies or tribes that were completely unaware of each other meet, Mauss tells us, they have only two choices: "confide in each other or absolutely challenge each other. If one confides, one must give everything and accept all demands—the most expensive goods, weapons, women, children, words." Everything that is demanded must be given immediately, to signify that one makes an unconditional bet on the alliance, without which everyone immediately relapses into war. It is only once this unconditional bet on the alliance has been accepted, and once it has been consolidated and instituted, that the accounts can begin to be drawn up. And in archaic society, in fact, people spend their time accounting for the value of goods that are given. There is an amount of tit for tat, of utilitarian calculation. Everything is weighed, everything is measured, but within the framework of this general unconditionality. If this first unconditionality does not benefit one

party, then the party renounces unconditionality. The political community falls apart and finds itself in a state of secession or civil war.

Only through this concept of conditional unconditionality[13] is it possible, I believe, to fully understand the nature of the gift analyzed by Mauss. For some, Jacques Derrida, for example, this gift is anything but a gift, since it calls for a countergift and is loaded with different forms of interest. In a word, it is not altruistic and sacrificial enough to be truly a gift. For others, Pierre Bourdieu, for example, it still masks its dimensions of exchange too much. The truth is that the gift is on both sides at once. It is not by chance that to characterize it Mauss speaks sometimes of *gift-exchange* and sometimes of *exchange-gift*. It is indeed both a gift and an exchange, a gift on the side of unconditionality and an exchange on the side of conditionality. If it has social and historical effectiveness, it is only because of this duality.

From the paradigm of limited gift to the paradigm of general gift

In a first article, written in 1960, "The norm of reciprocity," the famous American sociologist Alvin Gouldner established, in a very Maussian way, the universality of the norm of gift / return gift. Always and everywhere, the gift calls for a countergift. But in a second article, "The Importance of Something for Nothing" (1973), he rightly observed that in many situations where there is too much asymmetry between donor and donee, there cannot and should not be reciprocity. This is the case of the relationship of parents to their children, or of able-bodied adults to impotent old people, for example. There is no sense then for the donor to expect an equivalent return from the donee. He who finds himself at that moment sheltered from weakness and vulnerability must give unilaterally, without waiting for something in return. *Something for nothing.* The prevailing norm here is what Gouldner calls benevolence.[14] When we are in a state of fragility or vulnerability, someone has to be benevolent and caring. There must be somebody who cares. In a way, this article anticipates the theories of care that have emerged over the past twenty years, first in feminist debates, then in a whole series of other fields, in the wake of Carol Gilligan's book *In a Different Voice*, which was later extended, criticized, and systematized by Joan Tronto, in her *Moral Boundaries*. What these theories of care reveal is the central role of demand, starting with the demands for care and attention that stem from our fragility, especially as infants, patients, or elderly. But the question raised by these analyses is whether care and benevolence go beyond reciprocity. Apparently yes, since the one who receives is not in a condition to return. But the danger, as Mauss clearly shows, if there is no possible gift in return, is that the gift crushes the one who receives it, thus reducing them to impotence. We break this deadlock by reasoning in terms of an expanded gift, in the same way that Lévi-Strauss distinguishes between simple exchange and generalized exchange of women. In the expanded or generalized gift as in the generalized exchange, A gives to B who gives to C, who gives to D... who gives to A. Then the benevolent one, who provides the care, does not appear as a unilateral, asymmetrical donor, but as a donor who has received and will receive in turn from another. We move from the simple gift paradigm to the broader or generalized paradigm by introducing demand and the mutual asymmetry of donors and recipients.

3. This conditional unconditionality is cemented by the *political-religious* (the religious—*le religieux*—and the political—*le politique*). The gift establishes a triple alliance: *horizontal*, between warriors, who lay down their arms and decide by exchanging gifts to pass from war to peace; *longitudinal*, between generations, sealed by the gift of women (daughters, sisters), which allows the passage from infertility and death to life; and *vertical*, between humans and invisible entities. This third alliance is the locus of the religious-political. We must distinguish between, on the one hand, what happens within a given society in terms of politics (*la politique*), power struggles, religion (*la religion*), and economics, and, on the other hand, what is at stake at the society's borders, in the relationship the society maintains to its exteriority, which defines it in its specificity. Before something can happen *within* society, it must have been created, unconditionally, in a certain relationship to all that it is not, to its otherness. This creation, this instituting moment, constantly renewed and reiterated, is the result not of politics (*la politique*) and religion (*la religion*), but of *the political* and *the religious*, always intertwined—of the political religious.[15] The horizontal alliance between former enemies brings peace. The longitudinal alliance between generations, via women's fertility, brings life. The vertical alliance with the invisible generates chance, splendor, and the propitious.

The political, politics, and policies

The *political* can be thought of as the force instituting a political community or an established society; as the result of all decisions made by members of that community or society—to be allies rather than enemies or neutrals, to give and give themselves rather than oppose, defy, or ignore each other. But other political communities, other societies, other alliances would have been possible, were possible, at other scales, according to other modalities.[16] The *political* is therefore plural, like society itself, and it must not be identified with a given political community (and even less with the nation-state). Symmetrically, the concept of *politics* (*la politique*) only makes sense at a very high level of abstraction and generality. It too must be pluralized. In a first sense, it designates the field of instituted power, with its two sides: that of the struggle for power and that of the structuring of the apparatuses that make it possible to acquire, maintain, or increase it. *Politics*, in a second sense, refers to the interplay of actors within this field. In a third sense, the word refers to all the decisions taken by one political actor or another. Their *policies*.

A society can be defined by the conjunction of these three alliances, and thus by the integral of the gifts made or that are feasible between living members of that society, by those they make or receive from previous or future generations, as well as by those they make or receive from invisible entities.[17] It is instituted by revealing the share of unconditionality, and thus the sacredness, of these gifts.

Gifts are symbols, symbols of this triple alliance. Conversely, symbols speak and are valuable because they represent and commemorate those gifts that have moved from war to peace, from nothingness and death to life and fertility, from harmful and detrimental to profitable and propitious. In short, from diabolic to symbolic.

4. The enormous literature produced over the last fifty years on the prisoner's dilemma or the free rider attests that one cannot "rationally" make the choice of trust and cooperation. Subjects defined by the standard economic theory as "rational"—that is, thinking only of their own interest (let us leave aside the hypothesis of transitivity of preferences, which is, in reality, a secondary motive)—must necessarily distrust subjects they presuppose identical to themselves, since everyone knows that everyone (knows that everyone knows that everyone, and so on) will inevitably be prone to betrayal as soon as they find an opportunity to increase their personal satisfaction, and this is true whatever subtleties one instills in the formulation of the problem. As Durkheim expressed it, one cannot transform subjects defined as selfish into altruists. Not even in the long run. The choice of the gift, which is also, as we have seen, that of a certain founding unconditionality, cannot therefore be made "rationally." It supposes, at least, a leap out of the narrow field of utilitarian rationality. If it is nevertheless reasonable, however, it is because there is good reason to hope that the obligation to give back will be met and that if it is, everyone will benefit. So it goes, as we know, with the prisoner's dilemma.[18] A clever judge wanting two culprits to admit to their crime places each in an isolation cell and tells each

of them, for example, that if he denounces the other without being denounced by him he will be free; if he does not denounce but is denounced by the other, he will be sentenced to ten years; if both denounce they will each be sentenced to five years. And, finally, if neither denounces the other, each will be sentenced to only six months.

Let us summarize: If only the two prisoners agreed to trust one another, each would serve only six months in prison, instead of the five years each is going to face because each will have hoped to be acquitted by denouncing the other and will have feared that the other "rationally" made the same choice. The bet of cooperation would be a win-win bet for all, but it is made impossible by rationality.

On the other hand, the gamble of the gift, reasonable but irrational, or rather nonrationalist, has the virtue of creating a climate of possible *trust*, and therefore cooperation. Thanks to the gift, everyone feels grateful and in debt, positively, toward the others. And rightly so: since cooperation is beneficial to all, everyone receives in fact more than they give. The paradox, which sums up the whole paradox of the gift, is that the alliance must be aimed at for itself and not for the individual or material benefits it provides, because if one only wanted it for these reasons, then we would fall back into the field of instrumental rationality, into conditionalism, into *do ut des*, and the expected advantages of cooperation would immediately disappear with the gamble of confidence that, alone, had made it possible to switch from the diabolic to the symbolic.

Prisoner's dilemma, trust, positive mutual debt, and the paradox of the gift

The canonical formulation of the prisoner's dilemma, imagined by the political scientist Albert W. Tucker, is the following: two accomplices to a crime are incarcerated by a Machiavellian judge in conditions such that they cannot communicate with each other. The judge offers them the following deal: whoever denounces his accomplice will be released if the other does not denounce him, and the latter will serve ten years in prison. If neither of them denounces the other, they will each serve six months in prison. If they denounce each other, they will each serve five years in prison. The prisoner's dilemma demonstrates the collective irrationality of the individual instrumental rationality of the *Homo economicus*. Indeed, since neither prisoner trusts the other, the only "rational" solution is for them to denounce or accuse each other. They will then be sentenced to five years in prison, whereas they would only do six months if they trusted each other, in other words if they rejected instrumental rationality by betting that the other would do the same. Such a bet is of the order of the gift. And, conversely, any gift is like a bet on the generosity in return of the one who received the gift. By showing the trust one has or believes one should have in the other, one challenges the other to show his generosity in return and in turn trust the donor. The gift is therefore a trust operator. Once this climate of trust is established, everyone wins. Our two accomplices only serve six months each in prison. More generally, Jacques Godbout shows that what he calls a feeling of positive mutual debt prevails in the system of mutual giving. Each feels that the other gives more than he receives. The gift and trust bring such benefits that it is obviously tempting for a *Homo economicus* to be more or less strategic or cynical and to use them to his own advantage. To make very small donations to receive very large ones. Every good salesman knows the ropes. Which nevertheless have their limits, highlighted by Godbout again, in his commentary on Dale Carnegie's famous worldwide best seller, *How to Win Friends and Influence People* (1936). The title has clear utilitarian connotations. He suggests that the reader will find recipes to make useful friendships. To increase his social capital, we would say today. But the answer is far from being so clearly utilitarian: to make friends, explains Carnegie, you have to "really love them." Here we touch on the central paradox of gift and anti-utilitarianism. Yes, the donation can be profitable. It can be interesting to be disinterested. But for the gift to benefit the giver, for it to yield a form of interest, an interest rate on the gift in some way, it must have included a share of true unselfishness and not have been made for profit.[19]

A Theory of Social Action

Once this general theoretical framework has been established, it is possible to resume a whole series of central discussions in anthropology—which are not the subject of our discussion here—on the relationship between gift and sacrifice, gift and debt, and so on. Let us focus instead on the elements of a theory of action that can be deduced from Mauss's essay on the gift. Most visions of Man in the social sciences consider human subjects first and foremost as needy beings that are prey to scarcity. This is also the case for all those modern political ideologies holding that the fundamental problem of humanity is the scarcity of material means. It is to the exact extent that we are, or would be, beings of need that it becomes legitimate to generalize the model of the *Homo economicus*, which is none other than that of a human being constantly seeking to satisfy his individual needs, whether economic needs, or the need for power or prestige.

1. But what ethnology—and notably *The Gift*—as well as history, literature, and so on show us is, on the contrary, that what we desire above all is not so much to satisfy our needs as to be recognized. Here we come back to the tradition of Hegel in the *Encyclopedia of Philosophical Sciences* or *The Phenomenology of Spirit*, recently revived, notably, by Axel Honneth and Nancy Fraser. *The Gift*, with its insistence on the potlatch, presents a particularly striking form of the struggle for recognition and makes a strong contribution to the thesis of the desire (or struggle) for recognition.

This thesis is attractive but as such unsatisfactory. To say that we wish to be recognized remains indeed too vague, even if, like Honneth, and following certain texts of Hegel, one specifies and accounts for this desire using the desire to be loved, respected, and esteemed. The question remains what it is we want to see recognized (loved, respected, or valued) in us or from us. The answer that *The Gift* provides is that we wish to be recognized as donor subjects, as generous and/or generators, who have given or are likely to give something precious; that is, something that is desired or considered desirable by others. By generalizing here again, beyond what Mauss directly shows, it is possible to add that we wish to be recognized as participants in what the phenomenological tradition calls dona-tion (*Gegebenheit*[20])—that is, grace, graciousness, or charisma. The unconditioned and the unconditional. And to be recognized, it is necessary to add, by subjects, individual or collective, and by institutions, which are also recognized as donors, generous and/or generators, which are themselves participants of grace and charisma.

It remains to specify the modalities according to which this desire for recognition is exercised, to detail the motives for action and, at the same time, to specify the place held among them by this famous "interest," in which proponents of utilitarian or para-utilitarian theories want to see the only key, the alpha and the omega of all our behaviors.

Recognition, self-manifestation, and play: Toward a general gift paradigm

On this theme of recognition, in addition to the canonical texts of Hegel, Honneth, and Fraser mentioned here,[21] we can refer to the issue of the *Revue du MAUSS* dedicated to it.[22] It seems to me that a decisive breakthrough can be expected from the relationship between the paradigm of the gift and that of recognition in the perspective of a general sociology.[23] We can indeed show that, where political economy questions the determinants of the value of goods or merchandise, the great authors of the sociological tradition, without explicitly formulating it as such, have questioned the determinants of the value of individuals or groups (classes, nations, civilizations, etc.) and what makes this value recognized or, on the contrary, ignored. But, contrary to the Hegelian tradition that sees in the desire for recognition a human specificity—which would make it something truly human beyond animal needs—we must link the quest for recognition to the more general and vital will to manifest oneself (*Selbstdarstellung*), which Hannah Arendt placed at the heart of her sociological philosophy, and whose presence and strength the zoologist Adolf Portmann perceived in the animal world.[24] Here, we immediately encounter the question of *play*, this anti-utilitarian dimension par excellence of human action, which is perhaps only the other side of the gift. Or at least one of its essential components. It is not without reason that Johan Huizinga situated his famous essay, *Homo ludens*, in the immediate wake of Mauss's *The Gift*. Playing, giving: two ways of acting as if and doing "something else"—something other than useful, than the satisfaction of need and submission to necessity? Two ways to assert one's liberty and creativity?[25] Or, more simply and more generally, to experience the feeling of existing?[26]

Beyond the gift paradigm expanded by the integration of demand, of benevolence and care, a more general gift paradigm emerges, which takes into account donation, grace, charisma, recognition, and play.

2. The main problem with the "axiomatic of interest," in other words with all these theses, so numerous and multiform, which aim to explain all human activity by the sole force of self-interest "in the final analysis," is not that they are saying that the pursuit of self-interest is important—it undoubtedly is—but that they suggest that self-interest suffices, and that the other dimensions of action are only particular modalities of interest. Economists, for example, have no opposition to the idea that there can exist altruistic subjects as long as altruism is understood as a particular modality of selfishness. There would be individuals so constituted—estimated at 20% of the total population—that the only way for them to satisfy their own selfish interests would be to satisfy their altruistic inclinations. Economists will also readily acknowledge that there are pleasures in friendship, but they will harness them to a modality of shared interest or selfish altruism. Philosophers or economists inspired by utilitarianism are also aware that contracts, adopted out of personal convenience, can only be respected if a force superior to the contracting parties, such as law or morality, compels them to do so. But economists believe they can deduce the emergence of this superior force from a generalized calculation of individual best interests.

In Mauss, on the contrary, we see not one but four dimensions of action. Four irreducible primary motives, organized into two pairs of opposites. The first opposition shows that in all our actions there is, indeed, an element of personal interest or "self-interest." But there is also, just as much and just as originally, an element of interest in others, or altruism. Of "loving-ness" (*aimance*). And this taste for others, this sympathy, is not a subset or a result of self-interest. Interest in others exists from the earliest days of human existence as evidenced by studies of the development of imitation and reaction to others in infants. The second opposition shows that there is also an element of obligation in all our actions. On the one hand, a physical and biological obligation, and on the other, a social obligation, in which Durkheim saw the characteristic and constitutive trait of the social fact. We can't avoid celebrating Christmas, the kid's birthday, a colleague's retirement, obtaining a high school degree, looking for a job. There are so many social obligations that we can't avoid, or only with difficulty. But we can only fulfill these obligations if we bring in a measure of liberty and creativity. Just as in a game, where it is only by respecting the rules that you can become a good and inventive player.

These four motives—self-interest, interest in others, obligation, and liberty-creativity—are all equally primary and irreducible to each other. They are always mixed up in practice. And it is imperative that they be so, because they are "hybrids," as Mauss formulates it.[27] For if there existed only self-interest, there would only be war of all against all. If there were only interest in others—which fascist and communist regimes, or religious fanaticism, have exalted—then we would immediately enter a sacrificial regime. The self-sacrifice that allows the sacrifice of others. If there were only obligation, there would only be formalism, ritualism, and sterility. If, finally, there were only liberty, there would be nonsense, each of us devoted to the "gratuitous acts" of which Gide spoke in *The Vatican Cellars*.

Each of our actions must therefore include a certain mixture of self-interest, interest in others ("lovingness"), obligation, and liberty-creativity. Only a certain balance between these four motives leads to a felicitous action, to a right type of action, and guarantees a form of coherence of the subject, whether this subject is individual or collective. By detailing these four poles, by taking into account the influence that each of the poles exerts on its opposite, we obtain the following visualization:[28]

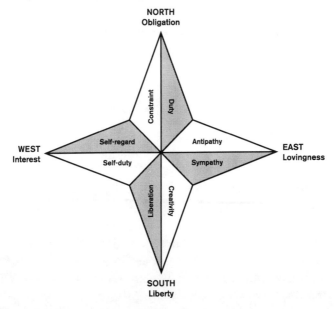

3. It is possible to generalize this theory of individual action to a *theory of collective action*. Or to a theory of what economists call coordination, and which refers to what Élie Halévy, in his attempt to define utilitarianism, called a theory of the harmonization of interests.

These interests can be coordinated by the contract, according to a logic of self-interest. This is what Halévy classified under the heading of *natural harmonization*, which one finds in all the theories of social contract and in the standard economic theory.

They can be coordinated by obligation; that is, by the law. By the *artificial harmonization* of interests, and we can think here of Bentham's utilitarianism, with its rational legislator, or of Plato and his philosopher king.

They can be harmonized, again, through sympathy or empathy. By interest in others or by lovingness (*aimance*). We are then in the register of what Halévy called the *spontaneous harmonization* of interests.

But the Maussian theory of action suggests that there is a fourth type of coordination, a form of harmonization of interests not identified by Halévy, based on the feeling of liberty-creativity, of a collective freedom exercised in common, which we can call *passionate harmonization*. This is what comes into play, for better or for worse, in all the effervescent moments of history, in the agitation of crowds, or groups-in-fusion, according to Sartre's term, in stadiums, in demonstrations, in insurrections, or, more peacefully, in concert halls, at the opera house, and so on. It is this passionate harmonization, moreover, that lies at the heart of the religious phenomena analyzed by Durkheim in *The Elementary Forms of Religious Life*.

4. How should we articulate the motives of individual action with the modalities of collective action? Probably by distinguishing four *registers of subjectivity* among which we arbitrate in every moment of our existence. Four registers defined by the type of recipient of the gifts we owe ourselves to make. As *individuals*, we owe it to ourselves alone. We give to ourselves and give of ourselves. But we are also *persons*, inserted in social relations with other persons via relationships of debts and mutual claims. We owe them and they owe us something. It is the register of concrete and personalized intersubjectivity. We are also and equally members of a politico-religious community, *citizen-believers*, in a relationship of symbolic participation with people whom we do not know, whom we will never meet, but with whom we feel in harmony as long as we share the same political and religious norms. We are indebted to the law that establishes this politico-religious community. And, finally, on a fourth level, we are *generic human beings*, similar to all human beings, worth no more and no less than them, and sharing with them the same primordial humanity.

In all our actions, we must oscillate between these four levels of subjectivity and establish to whom we must give: To ourselves? To our loved ones? To the political community? To humanity in general?

5. It must also be said that this gift relation is extraordinarily ambivalent and ambiguous, to such an extent that Mauss noted in his famous brief article "Gift, Gift" that in ancient Germanic languages the same word designates "giving" and "poison." The good and the bad. That which, depending on the dosage and the

intention, benefits or harms the recipient. This ambivalence is found in all Indo-European languages—in Greek with *dosis*, or in Latin with *potio*, for example. This means that you never really know who gives what. Is the true donor one who gives and also benefits from the advantageous position of the generous donor? Or is it not rather one who receives with gratitude and who, recognizing the other as a donor, constitutes him or her as an actual donor, since without this recognition of the gift, there is no gift? As for one who gives back: Does he or she really give back, or, in order to really reciprocate, must he or she not take the initiative of a new gift?

If for Mauss the gift relation is so dangerous and ambivalent, it is because those who are not able to give in return find themselves in a position inferior to that of the donor—they are obligated—and this leads them to lose face and even in some cases to fall into slavery. So, what is the donor's true hidden intention? To respond to the other's request, need, or desire? Or to assert one's own power and thus satisfy one's desire to be recognized as generous and generating? What is given, ultimately, in the gift: The thing itself? Its usefulness? Its property value? Or the intention that presides over it, the desire for an alliance, the value of a bond? Life? Rhythm? Vital energy? Mana? These are the questions that all the great religions and all the great moral systems will ask for millennia, asking what must be done so that the gift is real, is a true gift.

The Gift in History and Today

Mauss's merit is that he suggested that there exists a certain universality to the triple obligation of giving, receiving, and giving back, in which he rightly saw "the rock of eternal morality." But it is quite obvious that this universal is relative, since each society or each culture interprets it in its own way, namely by deciding who must give and who must receive what, and starting with the beginning, by defining the gifts to be made or received, by men and women, and by fathers and mothers.

1. It is therefore necessary to place the gift paradigm in the context of a sociohistorical vision. The main inspiration for the MAUSS in historical matters was Karl Polanyi. He dates the birth of the market—by which he means the "self-regulated market," disembedded from properly social rapports—to extraordinarily recent times, thus calling into question its historical universality.[29] In *The Great Transformation*, Polanyi explains that the market society—that is, the society that is embedded in the economy instead of the contrary, as it was before and everywhere else—emerged only in 1834, the date of the abolition in England of the Speenhamland system of poor relief (1795). There was no market economy, either—and therefore no *Homo economicus*—before the Hellenistic period in Greece or before the end of the Middle Ages, when, for the first time, local trade and international trade were brought together.

These dates, which are too rigid, can be discussed, and they are partly revised by Polanyi himself in posthumous texts. The market has appeared far more often and in far more places, and lasted for longer periods of time, than he thought. He is right, however, to insist that the market has been totally ignored or strongly contested and controlled, that it has not emerged—or has been subject to strong social and political regulation—in most parts of the globe and during very large portions of history. Almost everywhere *Homo economicus* and the market were perceived as having to be contained to avoid the breakdown of the social bond.

From the point of view of historical science, the unequalled epistemological model remains that of Max Weber (even if historians do not concern themselves with it most of the time...). If we really want to reflect seriously on the gift, we must, as Ilana Silber duly explained, cross Mauss's fundamental anthropological reflection with the historicization that the concepts of Weber's comparative historical sociology allow.[30] A general social science is to be built at the confluence of the Weberian tradition on the one hand, and the Maussian on the other, in a posture that reflexively transcends the limitations of the Marxist tradition.

2. What should we retain of the necessary historicization of the gift? First of all, that we are thinking about it after more or less two thousand years of Christian history and the *great universalist religions*. These great religions, as Camille Tarot suggested in a seminal article,[31] can be considered as transformations of the original system of the gift that extend the triple obligation of giving, receiving, and giving back (and explicitly add the request in the form of prayer) by (1) *universalizing*

it is the whole of social relations that can and must be viewed through the "lenses of the gift," to use Philippe Chanial's expression.[33] By way of illustration, I will mention two of the many fields in which the application of the gift paradigm has already begun to prove itself particularly fruitful.

The first is psychoanalysis. Let us remember, for example, and to remain in France, that the whole first wave of Lacanian psychoanalysis consisted essentially of a theory of recognition and of the place of the gift—even if most of Lacan's disciples tend to forget it. It can also be shown that what is at stake within analytical work is, fundamentally, a more or less controlled oscillation between the dimensions of unconditionality and conditionality that takes place through the mutual recognition of the analyst and the patient. It is a question of playing anew a failed relation of unconditional conditionality, because of an excess or a lack of unconditionality or conditionality, all of this through a subtle interplay between *believing in* (*croire en*, trusting the analyst), *believing that* (*croire que*, knowing), and *believing* (*croire à*, the hope of healing). Or, again, it is a matter of finally accessing one's own subjectivity in a rough balance between self-interest and interest in others on the one hand, and obligation and liberty-creativity, on the other.

Another possible application concerns the functioning of organizations. In the wake of Norbert Alter's beautiful book, *Donner et prendre: La coopération en entreprise*,[34] we find that all organizations face the same central problem: How to articulate the formal dimensions of the organization (the official division of labor, the allocation of tasks and of legitimate authority among the different services and functions) with its informal dimensions (the invisible face structured by primary sociality; that is, by all friendly or hostile relations among all the members and services of the organization)? The formal structure of an organization determines its *effectiveness*, the informal its *efficiency*. The efficiency of an organization stems from the articulation between a gift dimension and one of commitment (*adonnement*). The first dimension, that of the organizational social relation, is the one that weaves together the relations of gift and countergift between its members. We give each other useful tricks and know-how, precise information, psychological and emotional support. This is what binds us together in an organization in a permanent and generalized collective dialectic of self-interest and interest in others. The other dimension is that of commitment to work, to one's task and to the collective, which is played out through a subtle dialectic between obligation and liberty-creativity. The success (*l'efficace*) of an organization is the result of the articulation between its degree of effectiveness and its degree of efficiency. Between the dimension of secondary sociality and that of primary sociality.[35]

5. It is, however, necessary to go beyond this analysis of the relationship between primary and secondary sociality, because it is no longer as directly and simply relevant as in the 1990s. Over the last twenty years, in the wake of globalization, a third register of social relation has emerged that can be qualified as *tertiary* or *virtual sociality*. This defines the very peculiar type of reticular social relation that is manufactured through the Internet with a remote, intermittent, evanescent

sociality, where one can be at any time present, absent, connected or disconnected, involved or disengaged. Some see here the apotheosis of the gift, which the reticular multitudes exploited by cognitive capitalism would make triumphantly prevail. Others, to the contrary, denounce the gift's disappearance, hand in hand with the infinite multiplication and thus dissolution of identities in a second, third, or n+1 life, none of which is more real than the others.

If it is difficult to arbitrate between these opposing theses, it is because we have difficulty distinguishing between the third type of sociality that is emerging before our very eyes and its current neoliberal form. Let's go over this again. In a brutally ideal-typical manner it is possible to consider that humanity has until recently known two main types of society: the small and the large. The *small society* is an interconnected society, made up entirely of person-to-person relationships, structured, as we have seen, by the triple obligation of giving, receiving, and giving back. The *large society*, that of empires, civilizations, kingdoms, or republics, brings together, under the same politico-religious law and over large expanses, multitudes of people who do not know each other and have little chance of ever meeting, but who nevertheless recognize their solidarity through their subjection to a common law. Primary and secondary socialities are the forms that correspond to these two types of society. With globalization comes a third type of society, the *very large society*, or *world society*. The first society, the small society, functioned on symbolism (with the reversibility of gifts and symbols). The large society functioned because of the apparatus that was responsible for enforcing the law. The specific equip-ment of the very large society is the network.

But the network is also the privileged tool currently used by rentier and speculative capitalism set up under the aegis of neoliberal ideology. There is no evidence, however, that it cannot be used for other purposes. Large societies have been dictatorial or enlightened monarchical, theocratic or democratic. The very large society is, for the moment, capitalist and neoliberal, but it can easily—still relying on networks—become something quite different. Convivialist, for example (see below). Just as, in the large society, secondary sociality does not abolish primary sociality and the gift, so in the very large society the balance to be found is that which will allow primary sociality and respect for the law to have their due place. The network will then be at the service of interpersonal relations while preserving just the right amount of state and (nonspeculative) market, instead of contributing to their destruction.

6. What is stopping us from going in that direction? On the other hand: From what does speculative and rentier capitalism derive its power? From the colossal power of money and weapons, of course. But it is clear that this response is still insufficient. This form of capitalism would not sustain itself if it were not legitimized by neoliberal ideology and by the present difficulty in defining an alternative ideology that is plausible and as universalizable. Everything happens as if the impetus of any alternative political imagi-nation were stifled from the start. As if the field of the conceivable were now so closely marked out that

nothing other than the "moneymaking man"[36] can grow in its soil. A little bit like with GMOs.

To explain this impotence of thought, the most enlightening hypothesis is, in my opinion, that contemporary societies, at least in the rich countries, have gradually entered a sociopolitical form that is a complete novelty in history and, consequently, very difficult to identify. I propose to name this new socio-political form *inverted totalitarianism*, or *parcellitarism*. The history of the twentieth century was largely that of totalitarianisms and of the struggle to make democracy triumph over their seductive hold. The essential feature common to all totalitarianisms is the aspiration to (re)build a common, to meld all individuals into a great body, whether it be race, the state, or the proletariat. The individuals were nothing, the collective everything.

It is exactly the opposite formula that has triumphed in the last twenty or thirty years. Anything that relates to a common and to the attachment to some kind of constituted body is deemed illegitimate, archaic, and almost obscene. The categorical imperative has become that of unbinding. Everything must therefore be reduced to pieces, to elementary particles, whether it be companies, the state, knowledge, morals, or any institution. Indefinitely decomposable pieces that only recompose in new precarious and fleeting ensembles, the only ones adapted to the neoliberal norm of globalization. One could also speak of *globalized parcellitarism* (or *globalitarianism*). Neoliberalism is only the most visible ideological manifestation of this inverted totalitarianism, the one that emphasizes the importance of the economic dimension alone. But this general reduction of all social existence to the sole economic dimension is only possible because it is driven by a more powerful and encompassing dynamic: that of inverted totalitarianism. We thought we were done with yesterday's totalitarianisms. They are reborn in the paradoxical form of their inversion. But what was defeated and overcome yesterday can be defeated again today.[37]

Chapter 3
Ethical and Political Issues

Let us close the loop and ask ourselves what ethical and political conclusions can be drawn from all of the above, if we follow Durkheim's statement that "our research is not worth an hour's pain if it were to have only speculative interest." In closing, therefore, I would like to report on some of the MAUSS's ethical and political commitments. Those that translate the vocation of science *and* politics. All of them seem to me to share Mauss's inspiration when he committed himself alongside Jean Jaurès (whose right-hand man he once was, as it is too little known). Not by any a priori concern for fidelity, but, I would say, by a theoretical and ideological logic.

Some Commitments

1. The first great struggle of the MAUSS in its early years—that of the *Bulletin du MAUSS* (1982–88), notably under the pen of my friends Serge Latouche[38] and Gérald Berthoud—was in favor of a certain relativism, against the Westernization of the world and the Eurocentrism that so dominated in the 1980s.[39] This struggle is not obvious: What part of universalism should we preserve and what part should we leave to relativism? We still do not see this very clearly today, probably because this discussion brings us back to the question of how we should treat individuals, members of religious and political communities, and members of humanity in general. Generic humanity. What hierarchy should be established between these different levels of individual and collective subjectivity? According to what criteria? Latouche, after a period of nominalist hyperrelativism, came to plead for what he calls a pluriversalism. Perhaps not very far from what I called, some twenty years ago, a *relativistic universalism*. But as long as we do not specify which concrete policy choices all of this commits us to, these concepts remain too indeterminate.

The most advanced MAUSSian reflections on this issue are undoubtedly those developed by Francesco Fistetti in his book *Théories du multiculturalisme: Un parcours entre philosophie et sciences sociales*.[40] The crux of the problem probably lies in the fact that all human beings have a right, if we want to put it this way, to particularity as well as universality, to rootedness as well as uprootedness. Or, to act as persons and as citizen-believers inserted in concrete social relations that are more or less closed up, with an obligation of loyalty toward these social groups, and, conversely, to act as generic individuals or humans. The conclusion that can be drawn is that "the right political system is one that tends to promote the maximum cultural pluralism that is compatible with its own maintenance. Or again, which allows the highest possible degree of compatibility between the right to take root and the right to uproot, between the legal equality of cultures and de facto inequalities."[41]

Pluriversalism

The term "pluriversalism" was coined by Serge Latouche, inspired by Hindu-Catalan philosopher Raimon Panikkar's concept of pluriversum.[42] It is easy to see what's attractive about it. We cannot give up a certain universalism, but it certainly cannot be limited to a universalization of (only) Western values or notions. The paths of this universalism are therefore plural. This idea, seductive yet a little vague, can be clarified with the help of the important collection recently edited by Pierre Legendre, under the title *Un tour du monde des concepts* (A world tour of concepts), which looks at the translation problems in nine languages (e.g., Arabic, Chinese, Japanese) of nine concepts (e.g., society, state, contract, religion).[43] What emerges is that none of these notions is totally untranslatable, but that their translation often involves the invention of very approximate equivalents. Which say pretty much the same thing, but not really, sometimes even something else. In these translations, there is always a margin of error and some vagueness that opens the door to every

If we wished to congratulate ourselves, we could say that these positions anticipated those that we find today under the heading of postcolonial or subaltern studies.

2. The second important struggle of the MAUSS was in favor of an unconditional minimum income—which we called citizenship income—which seemed to us to constitute the logical completion of human rights.[44] This struggle, which preceded the introduction of the RMI[45] by two years, gained momentum in 1995–96 by bringing together some hundred well-known intellectuals—with people as diverse as André Gorz, Antonio Negri, Edgar Morin, Jean-Louis Laville, Jean-Marc Ferry, Patrick Viveret, René Passet, Robert Castel, and Denis Clerc—within the AECEP, Association pour une économie et une citoyenneté européennes plurielles (Association for a Plural European Economy and Citizenship), which had begun to Europeanize with the approval of other well-known intellectuals in Germany, Italy, and Great Britain. The agreement among these authors representing very diverse and sometimes even opposing ideological currents was reached on the shared certainty that we would not emerge from the mass unemployment that was beginning to take hold through either liberal measures of generalized deregulation or recourse to an administered economy. If these two solutions are not available, three interdependent proposals need to be articulated:

- accept that there are not enough full-time salaried jobs for everyone and thus redistribute them by reducing working time;

- develop to the maximum the sector of associations and the social and solidarity economy;
- create an unconditional minimum income that can be combined with other resources.

The call for these proposals, as I said, was beginning to gain some momentum in Europe when the "plural left" came to power in France in 1997, with Prime Minister Lionel Jospin, largely by chance, unexpectedly and without any program. The program that the "plural left" finally adopted was inspired in part by these proposals but without understanding their interdependence and by emptying them of their content. The reduction of working time, seen more as a means of combating unemployment than as a social choice, was more imposed and subsidized than negotiated and made open to the choice of plural lifestyles and a "revolution of chosen time."[46] Aid to associations was limited to the creation of unsustainable jobs for youth. And the introduction of an employment premium was preferred to that of a cumulative minimum income that would have made it possible to avoid the multiplication of unemployment traps. Ultimately, because they were based on the certainty that the norm is long-term growth on the order of 2 to 3% per annum, allowing for the maintenance of an institutional wage structure, all these reforms ended up protecting and favoring the holders of stable employment. And this, at the end of the day, was to the detriment of the precarious and those excluded from the world of work, both of whose numbers have not stopped growing since then. What made this policy credible at the time was the fact that growth actually returned for a year or two. One could therefore believe that the issue of unemployment was settled or was going to be settled. However, it came back in force with the 2008 crisis. It therefore remains necessary to update these proposals to make them the foundation of a post-growth-based society. A convivialist one.

3. Another battle was waged with a view to sustaining a general social science, in particular with the creation in Nanterre of so-called "modern humanities" diplomas, which included double degrees and double masters in sociology and economics (or econometrics) and sociology and history, all with a solid foundation of political philosophy and anthropology. Without aiming at an unobtainable transdisciplinarity, and by privileging a reasoned interdisciplinarity (on the model, in a certain way, of Mauss's "internation"), the bet was that one could marry two full disciplines in a university curriculum and that this radically changes things on the epistemological level (both in research and in teaching, or in the development of human beings and citizens). It would be necessary to analyze, in an idealist-typical way, the reasons why these diploma programs did not last in the end, in spite of the great pleasure and interest of the students. This is not the place to do that. It suffices to recall an obvious fact: everyone in France, no doubt more than anywhere else, is ardently and radically in favor of interdisciplinarity, except when it concerns their own discipline, which must absolutely be protected against any risk of impurity and defilement.

Convivialism

The latest battle to date, more topical than ever, is the one that resulted in the publication, in June 2013, of a small book entitled *Manifeste convivialiste: Déclaration d'interdépendence* (A convivialist manifesto: Declaration of interdependence), signed by sixty-four French and foreign intellectuals.[47] The first aim of this manifesto was to bring together people who belong to quite distant ideological spheres. Among them are representatives of the social and solidarity economy; those of ATTAC (Association for the Taxation of Financial Transactions and Aid to Citizens) and of the anti-globalist galaxy of the World Social Forums; the leaders of the Pacte Civique (Civic Pact), which brings together 130 left-wing Catholic-inspired associations; and the former Plan Commissioner Jean-Baptiste de Foucauld and Patrick Viveret, who believe that political change will require above all personal commitments in the fight against unemployment and corruption and for sustainable lifestyles based on frugal abundance. There were also Denis Clerc and Philippe Frémeaux, the founder and former director, respectively, of the well-known magazine *Alternatives économiques*; as well as the founders and animators of the *Appel des appels* movement, the psychoanalyst Roland Gori and the philosopher Barbara Cassin; and finally such unclassifiable intellectuals as Edgar Morin, Jean-Pierre Dupuy, Dominique Méda, Yann Moulier Boutang, and Serge Latouche. The most important point to put forward is that these renowned intellectuals, each with a vast national or international audience, agreed to discuss and sign a common text leaving what divides them in the background—including their respective egos.

The initial agreements

What brought such convergence to this meeting? The agreement, explicit or implicit, on at least six points:[48]

(1) First of all, and this was probably what was most decisive, a very strong sense of urgency. The certainty that we have little time left to avoid a whole series of disasters, whether climatic, environmental, economic, social, warlike, moral, cultural. Even if there is only one chance in a hundred or a thousand to avoid these perils, it is absolutely necessary to overcome sectarian squabbles and ego battles, the multiple narcissisms of small or medium differences, be they individual or organizational.

(2) The conviction that part of these perils results from the hegemony, both ideological and material, exercised throughout the world by a rentier and speculative capitalism that has become the main enemy of humanity and the planet, and which operates a paroxysmal incarnation of hubris and corruption.

(3) That, again, the first reason for the omnipotence of this rentier and speculative capitalism is the impotence of all those who suffer from it and aspire to another way of life, to perceive what they have in common, to name it, and to begin to give a plausible figure and form to their hopes. It is clear that everywhere in the world people are rising up, not only against misery but first and foremost against

the corruption of the elites and the dominant. From the Puerta del Sol to Maidan, passing through Tahrir Square or Gezi Park, from Aleppo to Bangkok or Caracas, it is an irresistible feeling of indignation that pushes people onto the street, sometimes with incredible courage. Revolt, it is said, is not enough to make a policy, and without a shared representation of practicable alternatives we quickly fall into the same rut. The generals succeed the generals and austerity succeeds austerity. Nevertheless, ideas or initiatives that shape the contours of another world are legion: "The defense of the rights of men and women, of the citizen, of the worker, of the unemployed, or of children; the social and solidarity economy with all its components: production or consumer cooperatives, mutualism, fair trade, parallel or complementary currencies, local exchange systems, the multiple mutual aid associations; the economy of the digital contribution (see Linux, Wikipedia etc.); de-growth and post-development; slow food, slow town, slow science movements; the demand for *buen vivir*, the assertion of the rights of nature and the praise of Pachamama; alter-globalization, political ecology, radical democracy, the Indignados, Occupy Wall Street; the search for alternative indicators of wealth, personal transformation movements, voluntary sobriety, frugal abundance, agrobiology, dialogue of civilizations, care theories, the new commons current..."[49] Imagine the strength that all these currents would represent if, in one way or another, they managed to oppose speculative neoliberalism together, and not just piecemeal and each in their own corner? What could possibly resist it?

(4) The certainty that we can no longer base our adherence on democratic values—and, a fortiori, universalize them by sharing them with countries or cultures that were or are still reluctant or distant—on the prospect of indefinite and significant growth in gross domestic product (GDP) and monetary purchasing power. Strong GDP growth will not return to the rich countries, for structural reasons, and it is therefore futile to expect from it, as all Western governments still do, the remedies to all our ills. And all the more vain, and dangerous, is that if by miracle this remedy were to be available again, it would generate other disasters, environmental, for instance. In any case, the planet will not be able to survive the generalization of the Western way of life, of the American way of life. It is not in the future but now that some days we can hardly breathe in Beijing or Seoul. And even in Paris, more and more frequently. Whatever one thinks of the intrinsic benefits or harms of money, monetary wealth, and GDP, it is clear that the post-neoliberal world we need to invent will be a post-growth-based world.

(5) The certainty, also, that what is most cruelly lacking for us to begin to build this post-growth world are not so much the proposals and sketches of technical, economic, and ecological solutions as an ideology, or a political philosophy, that is sufficiently general, shareable, and shared to allow for each of these propositions to find its due place within a coherent whole. The political ideologies of which we are the heirs—liberalism, socialism, communism, and anarchism—which we all combine each in our own way, in varying proportions (sometimes with the remains of religious traditions), no longer allow us to think about our past, the

present situation, and the possible and desirable future at the same time, as it is the role of political ideologies to allow. And this theoretical and ideological fatigue is another fundamental reason for our inability to think of ways to overcome neoliberalism.

What makes these four ideologies of modernity, if not obsolete, at the very least insufficient today? Two things, probably. The first is that, however universalist or cosmopolitan they may have been or wanted themselves to be in principle, they have always actually considered the emancipation they promised within the context of nation-states. We must be careful not to bury the latter too quickly, but they are not, or not any longer, on the scale of the—now clearly global—problems we are facing. The second, even more fundamental, reason is that all four shared the conviction that the most essential problem of humanity is that of material scarcity. Or, again, that humans are, above all, beings of (material) need. If this is indeed the case, then it must be inferred that humanity's number one problem is the economic problem, and that it is therefore natural for all societies, states, and governments today to subordinate all social life to the quest for economic efficiency and GDP growth. It is therefore not in these ideologies that we should seek help to develop a post-growth-based society.

(6) Finally, the certainty that the only hope of escaping in a civilized manner from all the threats that beset us is to deepen and radicalize the democratic ideal. This is a vast program, obviously demanding and complicated, since it is clear that it cannot be identified with the promise of material opulence for all, since it is a post-growth-based society that must be built, and

not with the indefinite multiplication of rights for all, since it is also a matter of combating illimitation and hubris. It will be necessary to limit at least the "right" to unlimited enrichment. But it would be too easy to suggest that hubris only strikes the evil capitalists or tyrants of the moment, and that it would not threaten ordinary men and women, who would be miraculously immune to it. Against the ravages of the aspiration to omnipotence, it will be necessary to balance new rights with duties and prohibitions. It is, therefore, in a different way, and in a different register from the indefinite multiplication of goods, services, and rights, that the realization of the democratic ideal must be considered. The general direction is probably as follows: where the inherited political ideologies placed their hopes either in the market or the state, the post-growth political ideology to come, convivialism, if this name gains currency, will place them in society itself, in the infinite myriad of actions undertaken jointly by citizens assembled for multiple purposes, in associations, if you will, and, more generally, in self-organized civil society. Or, better yet, in what Patrick Viveret rightly calls *civic society*. It is from this perspective that a new balance must be struck in finding rights and duties.

The agreements established in the "Convivialist Manifesto"

The drafting of the "Manifesto" resulted from roughly ten surprisingly friendly and constructive meetings, followed by numerous exchanges online that made it possible to clarify many points, to qualify certain formulations or, on the contrary, to harden others. The most central formulation, in any case the one that has generated the most exchanges and that can be said to represent the point of equilibrium for the group, is the one that presents convivialism as the thought of or search for "an art of living together (*con-vivere*) that values relationships and cooperation, and allows people to oppose each other without massacring each other, and while taking care of others and nature." A first formulation presented it more or less, and more dryly, as a philosophy of living together by making it possible to "oppose one another without massacring one another." "But why the need to oppose?" objected some. Others, on the contrary, would have liked to place more emphasis on conflict.

There was little discussion, however, on the five core questions and the four basic principles of conviviality.

Five questions:

- The moral question: What can individuals hope for and what should they forbid themselves?
- The political question: Which are the legitimate political communities?
- The ecological question: What can we take from nature and what should we give back?
- The economic question: How much material wealth can we produce while giving satisfactory answers to the moral, political, and ecological questions?
- The religious or spiritual question: everyone is free to add to the four previous questions, or not, the relation to the supernatural or the

invisible. Or, to put it another way, the question of meaning.

The "Manifesto" specifies that the only legitimate policy is one inspired by the four principles of common humanity, common sociality, individuation, and controlled opposition.

Principle of common humanity: beyond differences in skin color, nationality, language, culture, religion, wealth, and sex or sexual orientation, there is only one humanity, which must be respected in the person of each of its members.

Principle of common sociality: human beings are social beings for whom the greatest wealth is the richness of their social relationships.

Principle of individuation: with respect to these two first principles, the legitimate policy is that which allows everyone to assert their singular individuality in reaching their full potential, by developing their capacities, their power to be and to act without harming others, in the perspective of an equal freedom.

Principle of controlled opposition: because everyone has a vocation to manifest their singular individuality, it is natural that humans oppose each other. But it is only legitimate for them to do so as long as it does not endanger the framework of social community that makes this rivalry fruitful and not destructive. Good policy is therefore one that allows human beings to differentiate themselves by accepting and controlling conflict.

What contradicts these four principles, and at the same time prevents us from finding answers to the five main questions of living together, is the vicious circle that links, to varying degrees of proximity and connivance, hubris, corruption, the explosion of inequalities, rentier and speculative capitalism, tax havens, and organized crime.

Faced with this, the most universalizable strategy is the fight against corruption and inequality, the most concrete expression of which is the joint introduction of a principle of minimum and maximum income (or patrimony). No political community can be regarded as legitimate if it violates the principles of common humanity and common sociality by allowing large or small sections of the population to sink into abject poverty or, on the contrary, to rise to extreme wealth.

All these proposals are likely to generate very broad agreement. Too much, according to some, who will consider them far too general and indeterminate. But how can we hope to see powerful currents of world opinion emerge other than from a broad agreement on shared expectations? These proposals have to become effectively shared if they are to begin to have an impact on reality, and if anti-utilitarianism, the gift paradigm, and convivialism are to have anything other than, to use Durkheim's words, a "purely speculative interest."

Conclusion
The Ways of Anti-utilitarianism and Convivialism

Opposing rentier and speculative capitalism means opposing enormous amounts of wealth, of economic, financial, military, mediatic, and sometimes criminal power. On what weapons could a convivialist and anti-utilitarian movement count to face these formidable enemies? The first weapon, the one that is already at work everywhere, will be the feeling of indignation. But it will only contribute to real progress if, in all the places where it explodes and manifests itself, it is accompanied by the community's explicit awareness of comparable struggles being waged throughout the world, in all countries and in all types of activity. The primary goal of the "Convivialist Manifesto" is to propose a symbol, a common signifier allowing us, if successful, to name these struggles and to identify ourselves. Of course, these revolts will have to lead to a whole set of legal and political provisions, but nothing can be done in this direction if it is not preceded by enormous movements of public opinion and the mobilization of large masses. Shame, as the corollary of indignation, will also have its role to play. And perhaps, ultimately, the most decisive role. This feeling that there are things that are intolerable, that "you just don't do," because they violate common humanity, common sociality, common decency.

No historical change, no evolution, no revolution—political, social, or religious—has been possible, in fact, without members of the dominant strata rallying to the cause of the downtrodden by sacrificing their immediate interests, power, or prestige to higher interests, to the interests of common humanity and common sociality. Or, put simply, the interest of being able to look at oneself in the mirror without looking away. Perhaps, before even thinking about imposing any legal device, a convivialist movement in the process of internationalization should define a threshold beyond which extreme wealth seems morally indefensible. No one can exclude the probability that many of those who currently benefit (or believe they benefit) from this extreme wealth would then renounce it on their own and make this movement snowball.[50]

But at what level should we set the bar between poverty and misery, between permissible wealth and extreme wealth? In what form and under what conditions should minimum and maximum income be introduced? This depends, of course, on local situations, and on the outcome of citizens' debates. For the question to be asked, the principles and analyses presented in the "Manifesto" would have to begin to find representatives among political actors. We are far from that.

The work to be done, for the time being, is a work of conquering public opinion, a work of hegemony, as Gramsci understood it. And, even before the political question can be raised, it is necessary to be sure that the convivialist themes find echoes in civic society, since nothing will be done without that.

As I have said, the central proposal of the "Convivial Manifesto," which made it possible to reach an agreement between those who want to believe in the capacities of human cooperation and love, and those who, on the contrary, are more sensitive to the omnipresence of conflict, is borrowed from The Gift. This stipulates that the purpose of politics is to organize social relations in such a way that men can "oppose one another without massacring one another." Mauss added: "and give yourself without sacrificing yourself." The future will tell if this debate on a formulation borrowed from a scholarly work produces political effects. I earnestly hope it does. For what is neoliberalism, indeed, if not, theoretically and ideologically, the comet tail of a few political economy treatises? The MAUSS's bet is that sociology and anthropology, combined with political philosophy, can do much better.

PS: This book was written in 2014, six years ago. Of course, many things have occurred since, in the MAUSS and elsewhere. The only one I would like to mention here is the publication, in February 2020, of a *Second manifeste convivialiste: Pour un monde post-neo-liberal* (The second convivialist manifesto: Toward a post-neoliberal world), by Actes Sud. This second convivialist manifesto is signed by nearly three hundred intellectual personalities from thirty-three countries and is currently being translated into English (for the new journal *Civic Sociology*, from the University of California Press), German, and Italian. Other translations should soon appear in Japanese, Portuguese (Brazil), and Spanish, and later, I hope, Arabic. If it does not become really international, it is of no use. Our chances are small, I know. But we absolutely must try if we want something to be left of democracy and of the social sciences. ■

Endnotes

Chapter One

1. I explain my conception of sociology in much more detail in a set of texts gathered under the title *La Sociologie malgré tout* (Paris: Presses universitaires de Paris Nanterre, 2014).

2. Similarly, Norbert Elias, shortly before his death, deplored "the retreat of sociologists into the present" in *Theory, Culture & Society* vol. 4, no. 2–3 (London: SAGE, 1987), 223–247.

3. See Philippe Chanial, *La sociologie comme philosophie politique: Et réciproquement* (Paris: La Découverte, 2011).

4. Is a general sociology (a general social science) possible, or desirable? And how? Under what conditions? On this subject we can find the position of more than twenty sociologists, among them some of the most prominent in the world, in *Revue du MAUSS semestrielle*, no. 24 (2004), "Une théorie sociologique générale est-elle pensable?"partially translated in *European Journal of Social Theory* 2007, vol. 10, no. 2. See also Alain Caillé and Frederic Vandenberghe, *For a New Classic Sociology: A Proposition, Followed by a Debate* (London/New Delhi: Routledge, 2020).

5. I return to the idea of an unconditional minimum income below, when speaking of convivialism.

6. Christian Laval, *L'Ambition sociologique: Saint-Simon, Comte, Tocqueville, Marx, Durkheim, Weber* (Paris: La Découverte, 2002); Robert A. Nisbet, *The Sociological Tradition* (New York: Basic Books, 1966).

7. On this point, see issue 22 of the *Revue du MAUSS semestrielle* (2003), on "Qu'est-ce que le religieux?" [What is the religious?]. This issue presents a very broad panorama of the various possible definitions of religion. A quite recent issue, *Revue du MAUSS*, no. 49 (2017), on "Religion: Le retour? Entre violence, marché et politique" [Religion: The return? Between violence, market, and politics], tackles the problem anew. See also in English: Alain Caillé, "New Theses on Religion." *Social Imaginaries* 3.2 (Bucharest: Zeta, 2017), 169–179 and "On the Religious Dimension: Toward a Grammar in the Key of Gift"in *Revue du MAUSS*, no. 49 (2017).

8. I have explained myself on this issue in many texts. See, for example, "Qu'est-ce qu'être anti-utilitariste? Entretien avec Jean-Pierre Cléro et Christian Lazzeri" [What is being anti-utilitarian? Interview with Jean-Pierre Cléro and Christian Lazzeri], *Cités*, no. 10 (2002).

9. I present my arguments on the utilitarianism of Plato in *Don, intérêt et désintéressement: Bourdieu, Mauss, Platon et quelques autres* (Paris: La Découverte, 1993). On the place of utilitarianism in the history of Western philosophy, see Alain Caillé, Christian Lazzeri, and Michel Senellart, eds., *Le bonheur et l'utile: Histoire raisonnée de la philosophie morale et politique* (Paris: La Découverte, 2001). On this topic, without knowing it, I rejoined Alvin Gouldner's *Enter Plato* (New York: Basic Books, 1965).

Chapter Two

10. Where we can find all the threads of what I call the gift paradigm. Taking into account the contexts and themes to be dealt with, I also call this the "political paradigm," the "paradigm of alliance," the "paradigm of symbolism," or even the "third paradigm," which is neither holistic nor individualistic but "interdependentist." I base this "interdependentism" on the model of Norbert Elias's sociology, and it echoes Georg Simmel's *Wechselwirkung* concept, which, it seems to me, is insufficiently rendered by the usual translation, "interaction." The idea of an effective *crossover* should be better expressed.

11. It is this set of transgenerational gifts that form tradition, the gift through time.

12. It is within the framework of this dialectic of the symbolic cycle of the gift and the diabolic cycle of taking that we must rethink the heritage of Marxism. See also on this point no. 34 of the *Revue du Mauss semestrielle, "Que faire, que penser de Marx aujourd'hui?"* [What to do with, what to think of Marx today?] (2009), and, more specifically therein, Alain Caillé and Sylvain Dzimira, "De Marx à Mauss, sans passer par de Maistre ni Maurras" [From Marx to Mauss, without passing through de Maistre or Maurras].

13. I put forward this concept of conditional unconditionality in *Anthropologie du don: Le tiers paradigm* [Anthropology of the gift: The third paradigm] (Paris: Desclée de Brouwer, 2000).

14. The relationship between Gouldner's two articles and the Maussian paradigm of giving is best explained by Philippe Chanial in his introduction to the collective volume *La société vue du don: Manuel de sociologie anti-utilitariste appliquée* [Society through the gift: Handbook of applied anti-utilitarian sociology], ed. Philippe Chanial (Paris: La Découverte, 2008). I develop the remarks presented in this box in an online article, "Don, care et santé," *Revue du MAUSS permanente*, May 9, 2014, www.journaldumauss.net/?Don-care-et-sante

15. For developments on the distinction among the religious, religion, and religiosity within a MAUSSian frame, in English, see François Gauthier, "A Three-Tier, Three-Level Model for the Study of Religion," in *Einheit und Differenz in der Religionswissenschaft: Standortbestimmungen mit Hilfe eines Mehr-Ebenen-Modells von Religion*, ed. Ansgar Jödicke and Karsten Lehmann (Würzburg: Ergon Verlag, 2016), 157–74.

16. The works of Bruno Latour and Alain Touraine, in particular, show that sociology can no longer be thought of as the science of society, because this notion only made full sense, particularly in France, as long as it evoked the unity of a sufficiently coherent, self-determined, and self-sufficient political community. Globalization shatters this representation. This does not mean, however, that the very concept of society should be discarded. It must not be abandoned but pluralized and dialectized, as François Dubet clearly shows in *Le travail des sociétés* [The work of societies] (Paris: Seuil, 2009).

17. The theme of the alliance with the invisible remains, to think about it, too restrictive. The alliance with the invisible must be placed within the framework of a more general alliance with the cosmos, the world, and/or nature. Milestones in this direction can be found in the Revue du MAUSS semestrielle, no. 42, "Que donne la nature? L'écologie par le don" (2013), which pleads for a "methodological animism."

18. Devised by Albert W. Tucker, in Princeton, in 1950.

19. Jacques T. Godbout, *Le don, la dette, l'identité: Homo donator vs. Homo œconomicus* [Gift, debt, identity: Homo donator vs. Homo economicus] (Paris: La Découverte, 2000).

20. In German, to say "there is," "there is something," one says "es gibt" (it gives), "es gibt etwas." So, it is very tempting to

think of all that exists naturally—nature, the air, life, and so on—as if it were given. Given by no one to no one in particular, but given all the same. In my last book, *Extensions du domaine du don* (Arles: Actes Sud, 2020), I defend the idea that if philosophers like Jacques Derrida or Jean-Luc Marion affirm that the gift is impossible—the "figure of the impossible"—it is because they think of the gift as if it should be a donation (something given by no one to no one, without any reason), whereas I contend, on the contrary, that we should think of donation (of nature, for instance), as if it were a gift, in the Maussian sense. Whence my plea for what I call a methodological animism.

21. See Axel Honneth, *The Struggle for Recognition*, trans. Joel Anderson (Cambridge: Polity, 1996); Nancy Fraser and Axel Honneth, *Recognition or Redistribution: A Political-Philosophical Exchange*, trans. Joel Golb, James Ingram, and Christiane Wilke (London: Verso, 2003). Before Honneth's text was published, the classical interpretation of Hegel's struggle for recognition was that given by Alexandre Kojève in his *Introduction to the Reading of Hegel*, trans. James H. Nichols (Ithaca: Cornell University Press, 1980), originally published as *Introduction à la lecture de Hegel* (Paris: Gallimard, 1947).

22. See the *Revue du MAUSS semestrielle*, no. 23, "De la reconnaissance: Don, identité and estime de soi" (2004). See also Paul Ricoeur, *Parcours de la reconnaissance* (Paris: Stock, 2005), Marcel Hénaff, *Le Prix de la vérité* (Paris: Seuil, 2002) and (in English) the text I wrote with Christian Lazzeri,"Recognition Today: The Theoretical, Ethical and Political Stakes of the Concept" in *Recognition, Work, Politics. New Directions in French Critical Theory*, ed. J. P. Deranty et al (Leiden: Brill, 2007), 89–125.

23. See Alain Caillé, "Reconnaissance et sociologie," in *La Quête de reconnaissance: Nouveau phénomène social total*, ed. Alain Caillé (Paris: La Découverte, 2007).

24. On this theme, I suggest Jacques Dewitte's beautiful book, *La manifestation de soi: Éléments d'une critique philosophique de l'utilitarisme* (Paris: La Découverte, 2010), and the republication of Adolf Portmann's book, *La forme animale*, with a preface by Dewitte (Paris: Éditions La Bibliothèque, 2013).

25. Roberte Hamayon recently brought important anthropological material to the reflection on play, which was largely left fallow since Johan Huizinga's *Homo ludens* and Roger Caillois's *Les jeux et les hommes*. See Hamayon, *Why We Play* (New York: Hau, 2015), originally published as *Jouer: Une étude anthropologique à partir d'exemples sibériens* (Paris: La Découverte, 2012). See also in English, Alain Caillé, "Playing/Giving," *Revue du MAUSS* no. 41(2013).

26. François Flahaut, *Le sentiment d'exister: Ce qui ne vas pas de soi* (Paris: Descartes, 2002).

27. At the end of the lecture from which I derived the present book, a discussion began with my friend and philosopher Christian Lazzeri, who objected that the thesis that there is a dimension of interest in others that cannot be reduced to self-interest is unfalsifiable; so we can't do without the concept of interest. On the contrary, I have been thinking for a very long time that it is precisely the axiomatic of interest that is radically unfalsifiable. Whatever we do, we can always say that it was done out of interest, since interest is precisely conceived as what motivates and triggers action. This is a variant of the sleeping virtue of opium. It is therefore very amusing to see Karl Popper, champion of the falsifiability criterion, defend this unfalsifiable model par excellence. No one can ever prove that we don't do things out of interest. I would tend to say, like Michel Terestchenko—in *Un si fragile vernis d'humanité: Banalité du mal, banalité du bien* (Paris: La Découverte, 2005)—that the burden of proof lies with those who want to see interest everywhere, and that they must explain to us what interest(s) they are talking about. Moreover, in *Théorie anti-utilitariste de l'action: Fragments d'une sociologie générale* (Paris: La Découverte, 2012), I rely in particular on ethological and neurological data to argue this irreducibility of interest in others to self-interest.

28. Developed, specified, and explained in Caillé, *Théorie anti-utilitariste de l'action*.

29. A vast debate might be conducted on this, particularly in connection with the best-selling book *Debt: The First 5,000 Years* (New York: Melville House, 2011), by David Graeber, who wrote extensively in the *Revue du MAUSS* and who questions, without sufficiently explaining himself, many Polanyian and even Maussian positions. For a reappraisal of Polanyi's

thought, see Alain Caillé and Jean-Louis Laville, "Actualité de Polanyi," afterword to Karl Polanyi, *Essais* (Paris: Seuil, 2008).

30. See Ilana Silber, "Mauss, Weber et les trajectoires historiques du don," *Revue du MAUSS semestrielle*, no. 36, "Marcel Mauss vivant" (2010). For a clear and systematic presentation of Weber's sociology, see Stephen Kalberg, *Max Weber's Comparative Historical Sociology: An Interpretation and Critique* (New York: Polity, 1993).

31. Camille Tarot, "Repères pour une histoire de la naissance de la grâce," *Revue du MAUSS semestrielle*, no. 1, "Ce que donner veut dire: Don et intérêt" (2003).

32. See, in particular, Chanial, *La société vue du don*.

33. Ibid.

34. Paris: La Découverte, 2009.

35. This analysis is developed and detailed in Alain Caillé and Jean-Édouard Grésy, *La révolution du don: Le management repensé à la lumière de l'anthropologie* (Paris: Seuil, 2014).

36. The reference here is to a text by Voltaire called the "man with forty crowns."—Trans.

37. On this notion of parcellitarism, see Alain Caillé, "Un totalitarisme démocratique? Non, le parcellitarisme" [A democratic totalitarianism? No, parcellitarism], in *Quelle démocratie voulons-nous? Pièces pour un débat* [What democracy do we want? Elements for a debate], ed. Alain Caillé (Paris: La Découverte, 2006).

Chapter Three

38. Serge Latouche is now widely known as the pope of the "de-growth" movement.

39. Gérald Berthoud, *Plaidoyer pour l'autre* (Geneva: Droz, 1982); Serge Latouche, *L'Occidentalisation du monde* (Paris: La Découverte, 1989), followed by *La Planète des naufragés* (Paris: La Découverte, 1991).

40. [Theories of Multiculturalism: A journey between philosophy and social science] (Paris: La Découverte, 2009), with an afterword by Alain Caillé and Philippe Chanial.

41. Ibid., 191.

42. See Raimon Panikkar, *Pluriversum: Pour une démocratie des cultures* (Paris: Les Éditions du Cerf, 2013), with a preface by Serge Latouche.

43. Pierre Legendre, ed., *Tour du monde des concepts* (Paris: Institut d'études avancées de Nantes / Fayard, 2013).

44. See also on this point *Le Bulletin du MAUSS*, no. 23, "Du revenu social: Au-delà de l'aide, la citoyenneté" (September 1987), and *La Revue du MAUSS semestrielle*, no. 7, "Vers un revenu minimum inconditionnel" (1996).

45. The French social security program, literally "minimum insertion income."

46. Heralded by Jacques Delors and his followers, particularly Jean-Baptiste de Foucauld.

47. Lormont: Le Bord de l'Eau, 2013. I say nothing here about two other important struggles: (1) In the wake of the struggle to create generalist social science degrees at Nanterre, the MAUSS has constantly called for a reintegration of economics into the field of social sciences; see also *La Revue du MAUSS semestrielle*, no. 30, "Vers une autre science économique (et donc un autre monde)" (2007). These efforts were not in vain and resulted in the creation of the Association française d'économie politique, which brings together six hundred university or para-university economists, and which actively campaigns for the creation of an academic recruitment section within the Conseil national des universités, entitled Économie et sciences sociales. (2) Another important mobilization consisted of the attempt to save what can be saved of the French university (more threatened than the universities of other countries because of its structural separation from the Grandes Écoles—large, medium, or small but increasingly private and expensive—and the CNRS; see also *La Revue du MAUSS*, no. 33, "L'Université en crise: Mort ou résurrection" (2009), which led to the constitution of the group known as the "refounders," bringing together academics from a very broad ideological spectrum—from the extreme left to the center right—united by opposition to government elites or teachers' unions, right or left, who all refuse to see what is evident, the downgrading of the French university system.

48. I repeat here part of the introduction to no. 43 of *La Revue du MAUSS semestrielle* (2014), "Du convivialisme comme volonté et comme espérance."

49. I quote here from the "Convivialist Manifesto."

Conclusion

50. Of course, some of our friends have remained skeptical, as will surely many of our readers, in the face of this call for moral indignation. As an example of the potential power of this weapon, one can recall Gandhi's nonviolence, or the surprising fact reported by Hannah Arendt in *Eichmann in Jerusalem*: not a single Danish Jew was deported under Nazi occupation, because the Danes responded to every German request with "We don't do things like that here."

Also available from Prickly Paradigm Press:

continued